A Heart for GED: Instructors Speak

TAKE ACTION! Publishing

Funny, Scary & Inspirational Stories
shared by ABE/GED Instructors

Various Authors

A Heart for GED: Instructors Speak
Copyright © 2019 TAKE ACTION! Publishing

ISBN: 978-0-692-06599-0

TAKE ACTION! Publishing
http://takeactionpublishing.blogspot.com

ISBN 978-0-692-06599-0
90000

9 780692 065990

This book is dedicated to the thousands of men and women around the world who teach ABE/GED classes to adult learners. Thank YOU for your passion, your service and your heart for GED!

Table of Contents

Chapter 1

FAFSA: Free Application for Financial Student Aid or How Hard Was Your Life?

GED Class: Hannah and Jessica – Algebra, pg. 72, 74. Fill out FAFSA.

It seemed like a pretty easy day until I realized when I filled out my own FAFSA my dad sat next to me at the computer in my family's house. He practically did the whole thing for me because he wanted to make sure it was correct and because I became exasperated after question 80.

Needless to say, when I looked at my To-Do sheet that day, I got that panic feeling and began to wonder, "How are we going to do this?"

When the girls came in and we began fill out the form, it wasn't that difficult. Your name, address, marital status, and the highest grade your parents had completed. Even the last blank didn't prove to be too personal.

However, the brows began to furrow and the questions began to multiply as we turned the page to determine "Student Dependency Status." This is also when the stories of my students' lives began to unfold.

Do you have children who will receive more than half of their support from you between July 1, 2009 and June 30, 2010? (Q53)

Jessica had a daughter, but her husband, a coal miner, was the one who provided the income for the family. This was one of the primary reasons Jessica wanted to get her GED, "to have the ability to apply for a well-paid job or in case something happened to her marriage," as she put it.

Do you have dependents (other than your children or spouse) who live with you and who receive more than half their support from you, now through June 30, 2010? (Q54)

Hannah often talked about her crowded house and gave it as one of the reasons she was not successful in a traditional high school setting. Her house was the home to her mommy and daddy – both unemployed; her papa – who was quite sick; her 5-year-old sister and any friends her mother decided to let into the house. Hannah couldn't wait to have a place of her own. While she was taking GED classes, she worked long hours at the local Dairy Queen.

At any time since you turned age 13, were both your parents deceased, were you in foster care or were you a dependent or ward of the court? (Q55)

"Why do they ask these questions?" Jessica asked.

Hannah quickly responded, "They want to know how hard your life was, so the harder your life is the more money you get."

I smiled. I guess she had a point.

"Well, see, I don't know how to answer these questions," Jessica said, while nervously pulling her hair back and looking down. "See, when I was living in Ohio, we moved down here and I wasn't living with my mom. I was living with other people."

"Were you in foster care?" I asked, surprisingly comfortably.

"No, I was living with my aunt and then my cousin and just moving around a lot and they didn't really take good care of the papers. My mom might have them, but I really don't want to go over there and get them. Do you think I'll have to go over there and get them?" Jessica asked with panicked eyes. Jessica - with her beautiful hair, manicured nails, desire to be proper, and her intelligence - was tossed around? She was unwanted? It wasn't the story I imagined for her, and she hid it well. I was sure there had to be a way around getting the papers.

"Don't worry, Jess," I said. "You won't have to go get the papers."

Written by Shannon Hoffman

HOW I LEARNED TO STOP FOLLOWING THE RULES SO CLOSELY AND RENEWED MY FAITH IN SANTA

I have always been a believer in the power of following the directions. I'm no tyrant but I have always felt that following the rules is very important. No rules and things eventually erupt into chaos and then, where would we be?

Come to my house and you will find a drawer full of service directions for every appliance I've ever owned. Before we play any board game, I feel this overwhelming need to reread the rules aloud to my family. Nobody can suck the fun right out of a game of UNO like me! You get the picture, right? When I was offered a job as the ABE Instructor for the Clinical Care Unit at Iowa State Penitentiary, I accepted it with a mixture of excitement and trepidation.

My worries were soon eased as I attended my first day of training and received the Policy and Procedures book. If you are a lover of rules like me, prison just might be the place for you.

I headed into my new classroom protected by this massive shield of regulations. If anything should go wrong, I would have the rules to set things back to right.

My class, comprised of eight students and myself at any given time, varied in range not only in the cognitive ability of the students but in mental disorders as well. I could have a 50-year-old illiterate gentleman with moderate mental retardation sitting next to a 22-year-old gentleman who had to drop out of school in the eleventh grade due to the symptoms of his burgeoning schizophrenia.

On this particular morning I was helping "Mr. E" read through the directions for his assignment. He was to circle the people who were "real" and underline the people who were "not real." We decided to do the first few together, and I asked him what the first picture was.

"A fireman?" he asked.

"Correct. Is he real or not real?" I asked.

"Real" he replied and he circled the picture.

"How about this next picture?" I asked.

"A teacher?" he answered.

"Very good Mr. E. What should you do with her picture?" I asked.

"Circle it!" he said with a smile of accomplishment.

"Great Mr. E, I think you're getting it." I said.

He studied the next picture for a few seconds and said "An elf?" I answered yes and asked him what he should do with the picture.

"Circle it!" he reported.

"Wait a minute Mr. E. We don't want to circle it because elves aren't real."

It was then I heard the squeal of an overtaxed chair scooting out from under a desk behind me. I turned to see "Mr. B," a man who is so big he causes a cranial eclipse every time he passes between the sun and me, angrily turn to face me.

"Mr. Murray! Elves are so real! They're the ones who help Santa at the North Pole!" he yelled before taking a step towards me.

I realize now that it was the rattle of shackles out in the hall, but at the time I could have sworn I heard Santa's sleigh bells ringing in the distance.

With a complete disregard for the directions I replied, "You know Mr. E, I forgot about them. I think you better circle the elf." Mr. B returned to his seat, Mr. E aced his assignment, and I lived to see another Christmas.

Written by Kerry Murray

A FAMILY TO REMEMBER

Several years ago while I was working in adult literacy, Eddie C. came to me wanting to learn how to read. It was quite obvious that he needed help. He was a slender man looking no more than to be in his late twenties. As he slowly began to tell me why it was important for him to become a reader, I realized that he was quite a courageous young man to seek the help that he needed.

I had previously taught Reading Recovery in the adjoining town where he lived and upon asking him if he had children, I was taken back to find out that he had four children who were in that adjoining town's school system. His four children, although I didn't know it at the time had been in the Reading Recovery Program where I taught. I remembered how everyone always wondered why their mother and father never came to parent-teacher conferences. Many attempts were made to contact the parents but to no avail. It was our conclusion that the children had no support at home.

Now, here he was—the father of the four children who were in the Reading Recovery Program. I not only had the chance to help him become literate, but I also helped him learn how to help his children with their reading.

The remediation with Eddie C. began with letter knowledge. Eddie was quick to make the sound/symbol connections. He soon began to blend sounds together to make words. He was proud of his progress and so was I. He began to feel confident in his ability to monitor his reading and soon caught on to the use of cross checking for meaning, visual, and structural cues. His four children finally had a father who understood that they needed to become readers. Progress continued, and it was an overwhelming delight to be a part of that progress!

I think of Eddie C. often when parents do not show up for parent-teacher conferences. I wonder whether any of these other parents need the same type of literacy help that Eddie C. so courageously sought.

Eddie C. stopped coming one day, and I never saw him after that but it gives me a warm feeling to know that this family got the help they needed. As a result, everyone was a little better off for it.

Anonymous

SPRING 2016: *Ups, Downs, and Turn-Arounds*

I am so proud of one of my satellite adult literacy classes. Out of seven students, five came every Tuesday and Thursday and four of them are getting their high school diplomas. I am so happy for them, an experience I haven't had in seven years since working at other satellite sites.

I have watched these students grow, and I have encouraged them. I felt the doubt, but we overcame the doubts and now they are testing. Two of them have passed already. Two of them will pass tomorrow – the math. They all will have their high school diplomas.

One of my saddest points this season is a situation with a student on-site at a different satellite adult literacy class where I teach. I have enjoyed working there, and I have enjoyed the students there. The sad point for me is that a young lady last year at this time was pregnant. We enjoyed that experience with her only to find out that she is pregnant again. This hurts me because if this young lady doesn't turn this around I can see her – and I hope I am wrong – with several kids in the future and never getting her high school diploma. I can see her always singing that sad song about not getting a job and not being able to take care of her family. Those things just hurt me. I hope I am wrong. I want to be wrong. I am sad for her and sad for myself. I wish I could have done things a little differently, maybe it would have encouraged her to be different.

Overall, Spring 2016 has been a very rewarding teaching experience for me. I have seen a lot of students grow at two of my adult sites. One site is at a high school, and I have seen growth in my students there. However, I have especially seen growth in my Monday class here at the adult literacy organization where I am employed to teach. One of the challenges for me in that class is that I am not a Special Ed teacher, and I have two or three students in that class who are really special needs learners. I just don't know how to reach them, but I keep encouraging them to come. I have seen a little growth, maybe not as much as I like. I hope they continue to be part of this program. I hope we can meet their needs with a different instructor.

This has been a rewarding experience this year, and I am grateful to be able to be in this position to help change lives for so many young folks.

Shared orally by John Smith

Chapter 2

THEN THERE WAS DAVE

How can I choose just one person who inspired me? With over 20 fulfilling years in adult education, limiting my choice to one person is a real challenge. Every learner has a story, and every learner has had to overcome barriers. However, one inspirational learner I met was Dave.

Dave was a participant in a GED class I was offering to 15 students. He appeared self-confident and focused. Dave worked well in class and always had time to help other students. Sounds like the perfect student, right? And he was - which just increased my curiosity about him. How did he get here? I was soon to find out.

One day I asked the class to write an essay on a turning point in their lives. After the initial moans and groans about writing an essay, everyone started the project. All the stories were very similar to ones I had read before. All, that is, except one student – Dave.

Dave wrote that he was not a good student in high school. He wanted lots of money he said and didn't see education as a route to it. He left school and with the help of friends, he was able to start a small business. The business grew, and success was his. Dave had everything going for him. He had his own business, money in the bank, a car, and a gorgeous fiancée.

One night Dave and his friends were sitting in his car outside a local tavern when a bouncer unceremoniously threw a "drunk" out on the street. They watched the man helplessly try to stand up again and again, only to land on his face.

"What a loser!" Dave and his friends jeered.

"That will never happen to me," laughed Dave. He was invincible, or so he thought.

Over the next few years, Dave remained cocksure of himself. He started to use drugs, but he wasn't worried about being addicted. He was in control. He had everything. Then one morning, he woke up in jail. He'd been found lying in the street, stoned out of his mind. He had hit rock bottom. Along the way, he had lost his business, his wife, everything.

Dave went into rehab. During one group session, he noticed a man who looked familiar. Then he recognized him. It was the same man the bouncer threw out onto the street so many years ago – the same man Dave said he would never become.

This was a turning point in Dave's life. Dave got his GED, and I never expected to hear from him again. But, like I said, Dave was unique.

One morning about three years later, I was called to the phone.

"This is Dave," said the voice on the other end of the phone. "I was thinking you might be wondering what happens to students after they finish your course. I just wanted to let you know I will soon be graduating with my degree in English – but it won't be my last degree."

It is one thing to gain success, and then lose it, but to start over again, without bitterness and reach your dreams –

that is an inspiration.

I haven't heard from Dave since then, but I just know he succeeded in getting that other degree.

Written by Hannah M. Mills

RECONCILIATION

"Well, you may not end illiteracy, but you can make a difference in someone's life," declared my literacy trainer at the end of our first class. A bucket of ice water had just been thrown over my burning desire to change the world of ignorance single-handedly.

My first student has a smile that could melt the hardest of hearts. But, I wonder, is he trying to hide something? And how does he manage to keep such a radiant face in spite of the school of hard knocks he is currently enrolled? After all, what has he got to feel so happy about I ask myself in my "cellar voice." Homeless until recently, still unemployed, and reading at the level of a six-year-old child, this student is plagued by many of society's unsolved problems. These issues cling to the pores of his skin choking any reason he might have to expect significant improvements in his life. So why is he sitting there, hoping against hope that one or two hours of tutoring a week can matter?

During our first meeting, he mentions that thanks to his two previous tutors, he already has two different reading books, one at the kindergarten level and the other at the first-grade. My bewilderment is only heightened when he describes them. One of his tutors he calls laconically, "a lady in Washington," implying that he learned very little with her. The other he names as Andrew, adding, "Andy was white, but he was nice. Sometimes he fell asleep." Then with eyes gleaming mischievously, he asks me,

"You're not going to go to sleep like Andy did, are you?" I try to turn my amazement into a joke: "If I happen to doze off, just poke me in the ribs with your elbow." Then, this student of mine begins to tell me how little support he finds at home; my doubts grow.

"I can't get no help with this homework the computer lab teacher gave me. I asked my brother-in-law to help, and he said he'd help; he'd buy me some food. One of my nephews doesn't want to help. He says I should have learned all this a long time ago. My other nephew does the work for me. He doesn't wait for me like you do. He says I'm too slow. And I buy things for them! And my sister says I should get help from my teacher. Well, that's family for you!" he shared.

Still, nothing seems to trouble his firm belief that he will succeed. At the beginning of another session, he states proudly with a cheerful smile, "I called my father this Christmas, and I told him I knew how to spell his name: N-E-D. He laughed." This student like so many others in the world of adult literacy is a diamond in the rough.

The real questions linger under the surface for many adult literacy instructors and tutors like me: What are we looking for? What is our student looking for? How can we bridge the gap together?

Written by Charles F. Sleeth

A DIFFERENT KIND OF GIFT

My students give me gifts throughout the year. They don't realize it, but their perseverance, their triumphs over difficult personal situations and the joy on their faces when a concept is mastered – all inspire me to keep going. They're the kind of rewards that no one can spend out or lose.

When Christmas comes around, I feel uneasy when students say they want to buy me a gift. I teach in a poor area, and many of my students are struggling. I assure them that they are my gifts; their successes bring me happiness. I feel like a proud mother when they walk across the stage at graduation. Even so, a few gifts find their way to my hands, and I am humbled and grateful. One year, I even received a yellow card with no envelope. The student who gave me the card changed the signature in the card to her own signature. I cherish all of these things.

This year, my most special gift came from a lovely young woman who had worked long and hard to climb the GED level. With quiet determination and a winning smile, Felicia has evolved into a confident student who now sees community college as part of her future. When she first entered the class, she was painfully quiet and lacked self-confidence. Felicia shared that she "didn't know anything" and teachers "didn't bother with students in her school." When this adult education class showed her exactly how capable she was, a new person began to emerge. It was due to this change that my story came about. I've never really contemplated what the students think of me as a person. I didn't expect that they be curious about my life only that they want good teaching. Apparently, they wonder about quite a lot!

Felicia had asked me several times if I would be present on the last day of class before the holiday break. I assured her I would, and she gave me a shy smile and nodded her head. I was pretty sure that meant a gift was in order.

When the big day finally came, I entered the room early to set up. There she was beaming from hear seat in the back of the room and fingering a small purple box. I smiled and tried to be nonchalant. When I approached her seat, Felicia's smile widened.

"This is for you," she said quietly. Tapped to the little box was a ragged piece of newsprint. It had the traditional "To" and "From" written on it along with hand-drawn snowflakes along the edges. Just seeing it, made me want to cry.

I thought about the sacrifices it took to buy this gift. Working part-time at a jewelry kiosk, this young woman shared a studio apartment and was trying to make it on her own. If the thoughtfulness, itself, was a treasure, the conversation that followed was priceless.

The box revealed a pair of large, heart-shaped "diamond" earrings. I oohed and awed at the sparkly gift, and told Felicia that she shouldn't have done it. "Don't worry; they're not real. I got them where I work," she confided. "I get a discount, so they weren't much money." My heart was already melting when she leaned in conspiratorially and whispered, "I know they make you dress like that because you're a teacher." She waved a hand over me in assessment. I opened my mouth to reply but nothing came out. I bit back a grin.

"Well, I do get dressed up for parties," I replied, "and these are so festive and pretty, I can't wait to wear them."

Her eyes widened, and she leaned back as if to take this in.

"You party?" she shrieked.

With the generation gap firmly in place, I explained that my husband and I sometimes go to holiday dinner parties. She seemed disappointed in my response. Undaunted, she continued to explain.

"I knew you couldn't wear stuff like I do with all the bangles and stuff. They are for young people."

"Hey, you really know how to make me feel good," I kidded.

Felicia was sincere as she tried to make amends.

"When I get old ..."

YES, that's what she said!

"I'm gonna cover up and dress like you do, and I'll probably wear those little earrings, too."

OUCH! It was funny and innocent, but I didn't know whether to laugh or cry. Is that what they think? I'm old? My mind began to percolate about what folks saw in me.

I cringed as I remembered teachers who seemed like "for

the home." Year later, I realized that they were not even middle-aged. I began to recall things my students had asked me, and I had to smile. They had questioned my choice of "a ride." Their brows knit when I talked about Civil Rights or Viet Nam. I had become my idea of an old teacher!

I'm not quite ready to wear that title yet! However, I do realize that perception is our reality and the chasm between the ages of 19 and 50 had come alive for me.

Every time I wear my earrings, Felicia's smile is another gift. The story of the conversation has provided smiles and laughter. It's helped me not to take myself or my wrinkles too seriously, and I am proud to be that old GED teacher in Room 209.

Written by Carol McDonnell

THE PLUCKIEST STUDENT:
NO CHALLENGE TOO LARGE

Not fifteen minutes after her mother's arrest, the boyfriend flung Juanita, her three-year-old son, Nigel, and a black trash bag full of miscellaneous items out the apartment door. It was 3 A.M. on a cold night in New York City. Juanita grabbed little Nigel and hurried up the street to the church on the corner.

She had not really noticed the church in the past, but she took a long look at it now. The building was old, but it seemed to offer a safe haven. As she neared the church, there was a warm glow emitting from one of its round windows. With slight trepidation, Juanita pushed forward and grasped the handle of the large, heavy doors. She stepped inside the sanctuary.

No one appeared to greet them. Even after several minutes, Juanita and Nigel were still alone in the sanctuary. Tired and frustrated, she pulled Nigel in her arms and snuggled with him on a pew next to their entire world which also served as their pillow. They both dozed off quickly. In the morning, they were awakened and escorted to the nearest homeless shelter.

Eight months later, Juanita and her young son arrived in New Bedford. She was able to qualify for an apartment in public housing. It was their first complete night's rest since being thrown out into the street. Several days later, Juanita showed up to my Pre-GED class, eager to learn.

I asked her to introduce herself to the rest of the class.

Juanita held up her hand at eye level and motioned the attentive pairs of fourteen eyes towards her pinky fingers.

"See the scars left when my extra fingers were removed?" Her eyes widened excitedly as her new classmates began asking questions.

"Are you a freak or something?"

"What happened to you?"

"Does it still hurt?"

Undaunted, Juanita explained to her new classmates that she was born with Fetal Alcohol Syndrome (FAS) and that she also had scars near her baby toes. I sat patiently as the class once again erupted into a flurry of discussions. I realized I knew nothing about FAS.

Except for the scars and intermittent short-term memory loss, there were no other signs that Juanita was any "different" than the other students in my class. I decided to do some research on my own to learn more about FAS. The literature I found underscored the importance of patience and consistency with FAS students.

Juanita's goals were "to get a driver's license, pass the GED, and become an EMT, in that exact order." She told me this during our first counseling session. Her radiant smile and voracious humor soon enamored everyone in the school. The class accepted her readily and graciously. Juanita was allowed the extra time she needed to learn basic concepts. She had to do every assignment repeatedly. As I gave the class increasingly more difficult math problems to solve, Juanita fell further and further behind.

One morning Juanita arrived late and disheveled to class. Her eyes glazed while looking over the day's assignment; she seemed lost. That was the day the FAS monster made its first appearance. She did not know who I was or why she was sitting in the classroom. She had no clue how to solve the most basic math problems. Her FAS had her thinking she was a student in the university's writing seminar and that she was late for that class.

Taking in the situation, I gave Juanita a clean composition book and directed her to a table in the back of the room. She spent the next four hours busily writing non-stop. The next day Juanita arrived early to class bubbling over with enthusiasm. She could not wait to tackle the math problems from what she believed to have been the day before. To say I was perplexed is an understatement.

The next time Juanita's FAS presented a problem happened at home. She had received a bag of beans from the community food pantry with written instructions to wash the beans before soaking them overnight. Being a good student of reading, she literally washed the beans with dish soap, left them to soak overnight, and then boiled them for several hours. Juanita and Nigel enjoyed healthy portions of the beans all weekend, but soon they both came down with stomach distress. Juanita missed several days of classes, which led to her becoming more frustrated, impatient, and stressed.

The pattern of random memory loss and absolute literal thought continued over the next thirteen months. Her assessment test scores were very sporadic ranging from very low to extremely high. Her home life was out of my control but in the classroom, I kept a close vigil over Juanita for signs of the FAS monster. We developed a signal that would stop her emotional outbursts, constant pacing, and combative attitude. When that system failed, I would allow her to write. If she insisted on doing everything like the rest of the class, I would give her a more simplified version of the work with concrete instructions. We had good days, bad days, and very bad days.

In an effort to help Juanita succeed on her driver's permit test, I prepared a lesson plan from the manual. For several days, the students and I quizzed her on the varying laws and traffic signs. She did not pass, and she failed the next three times she tried. I felt helpless watching Juanita's goals slip away as I watched her grow increasingly more depressed.

It wasn't until Juanita's poem was accepted for publication in a student journal that her downward spiral turned itself around. Though nervous, she read the poem to the audience at the celebration party. The next day, she passed the permit test and started her driving lessons.

Juanita was once again in control of her personal demon, the FAS. Her progress surged forward. She obtained a part-time job in a retail dress shop, and she began to save for a car. She finally registered for the GED Exam. Though the appearance of the FAS monster continued, Juanita managed to rally back. Each time she learned a little bit more about the syndrome and a little bit more about herself. I struggled to help her, and I learned a valuable lesson. In this instance, the teacher did not always know best. I also learned the meaning of plucky.

Written by Lin Morley Gautie

Chapter 3

POLLYANNA FROM THE PROJECTS

Her braids form snakes like coils along her scalp. She holds her shoulders straight and wears a red t-shirt with jeans. Handmade tattoos decorate her arms. When she enters the GED classroom, she makes a racket with her presence even though she is not loud and the floor is carpeted. The other students look up from their work. She is 30 years old and reminds me of a Mustang running through a canyon. We all try to catch her spirit.

LaVeta came from Chicago with her boyfriend. He found work at the meat plant here in town. She left her mother's home when she was twelve and has lived out on the streets since then. She spent time on stoops in the summer smoking, reading, drinking, and hustling one thing or another. Her mother was her model.

LeVeta had four children, but one of the twins died of cancer at the age of three. Two of her children lived in Chicago with her grandmother, and her sixteen year old son moved to Iowa with her. He dropped out of school to run the streets.

"He's grown anyway," she says.

One afternoon after class, LaVeta tells me she has to go to the dentist because she is experiencing pain in her jaw from an old bullet wound. A year ago when she lived in Chicago someone shot her and left her for dead in an alley.

She told me she was brought back from death more than once Not long afterward, I brought LaVeta a coat, a t-shirt, and a box of candy from New York City. She gave the chocolates to the class. After class she tells me she hasn't been to the dentist yet. She says she has to rock herself to sleep and when she sleeps she has bad dreams.

She is black, my daughter's age, and comes from the projects. I am white, 55 years old and come from a middle class life in Iowa. If Buddhism is right, LeVeta and I are one. Still, an invisible electric fence stands between us, preventing either of us from crossing to the other side. We mingle only among the fractions, angles, sums, and differences of our lives.

I drive her to a counselor. Her voice is rough from who she is and the bullet in her jaw. On our way there, she calls her boyfriend who does not believe she's with her teacher. I talk to him on the cell phone. When we get to the counselor's office, she casually picks up a magazine in the waiting room. Her name is called, and she goes willingly into the room.

On our way back, LaVeta calls her mom and tells her she has Post Traumatic Stress, a phrase the counselor used to explain the sleepless nights.

LeVeta comes to class for a month. Each day she teaches us a glad game. Reading comprehension is easy for her, so she aces her first GED Exam. She laughs, joyous words explode from her, and then she disappears.

Written by Carla Steffey

PROVIDING INSPIRATION

I have spent for the past 20 some years of my life teaching adults who wish to sit for the GED Examination. I have always said that this is a profession that I fell into by mistake, but do we really do anything by mistake? I think I ended up teaching adults because that is what I was intended to do. The experiences I had early in life have helped to shape me into the adult educator I am today. Also, sharing my experiences has come to serve as a source of motivation for my learners.

Unlike most educators, I do not have a degree in education. My Bachelor of Arts degree is in Social Science with an Area of Concentration in Political Science. My Masters of Science degree is in Criminal Justice. Throughout my undergraduate years, my sister tried to convince me to change my major to Education. I wasn't having it. I had no desire to teach anybody anything. Oh, but did I mention that my first Work-Study job was as a tutor in the college learning skills center.

But let's back up just a little bit. Before any of this could happen, I needed a high school diploma. I dropped out of school in the 10th grade and never gave it a second thought. After the birth of my 7th child, I was trying to relax one evening but was being annoyed by one child who kept asking me questions. I brushed her off finally by telling her to get out of my hair. This child, about six years old at the time, kept mumbling "Get out of her hair. Get out of her hair. How can I be in her hair, I'm all the way over here?" I never had to respond as her sister, a year older shouted, "Shut up girl, it's just an idiomatic expression!"

I didn't say a word. I just got up off of the couch, eased into the other room and got the dictionary off the shelf. After looking up 'idiomatic' in the dictionary I returned to the couch and continued watching television. As soon as I took my children to school the next morning, I began looking for an adult education program.

This was late 1976. At that time, there were not a lot of adult programs around. The one I did find was Calvert Adult Education Center. The Calvert Adult Education Center was located 200 E. North Avenue in Baltimore City. This was the former home of Polytechnic High School and the current home of the Baltimore City Department of Education. The learning center was located on the 4th floor and students were not allowed to use the elevators. This in itself was probably not bad, but given the fact that I had just walked from northeast Baltimore, it was the pits. But, if you want something bad enough, you do what you need to do in order to get it.

I attended class at Calvert Adult Education Center for a few months until I was caught teaching the class. At that time I was forced to take the practice test and then the real actual GED Examination. Testing was done on the first floor, so I wasn't stressed from walking up four flights of steps. I may have even had bus fare those two Saturday mornings. It's been so long ago that I really don't remember. I do remember, however, asking my instructor for a written recommendation so that I could apply to nursing school. Yes, nursing school! But that's another story.

I guess I was feeling confident because I began applying to colleges long before I ever got any scores back. I was accepted to all of the colleges I applied to with the exception of Coppin State College. I was infuriated! How dare them! What was so important about this school that they hadn't accepted me yet? Well, it became my mission to get in there and I did! I was 1 of 3 students who got a Bachelor of Arts Degree in 1981 and graduated Magna Cum Laude. I returned to graduate at the top of my class in 1992. I tell people this story quite often and it serves to motivate my learners. After sharing this information with a student recently, he suddenly realized that he was not about to let an "old lady" out do him. Within one month, he had taken and passed all sections of the GED Examination and had begun applying to college.

I do let people know, however, that I got my Bachelor's degree to feed my children, but I got my Master's degree for me!

Written by Sandi L. Myrick-Nelson

MY MOST MEMORABLE MOMENT

While walking down the street one day, I met a former student who greeted me with a huge hug and a hearty "thanks." I asked myself, "What important lessons did this student learn from me?"

As an educator, I am not satisfied with how well my students can add one plus one or whether they can conjugate a verb correctly. I want to know if they are learning and passing on intrinsic values. I know my experiences have been rewarding and satisfying. Likewise, from them I have learned so much. Reflecting back, I would say my wish for them would be commitments for lifelong learning, a good value system and role model status for the youth of today.

First, a thirst for lifelong learning is a key to survival. Knowledge is the prime need of the moment. Taking full advantage of opportunities for learning and making use of the privileges in a living democracy will equip each student with a mental vision of health and education for years to come. As we look at our economic and political strengths, we must be more and more prepared for a better world tomorrow; therefore the better we prepare today means a more promising future.

Education doesn't stop with high school or college graduation nor does it stop at age 60. Education is ongoing and never ending. Today at the age of 60, I am pursuing a degree in Human Resource Management.

Next, values are institutions passed down from generation to generation. Teamwork and mentoring are vital in creating a value system started. Working in a diverse world with a diverse population will eliminate barriers and crumble obstacles. We must be vigilant in looking out for our fellow man. We must lend support to anyone or group that seek support. We must play a role in selecting leaders who are wise, courageous, and of great moral stature and ability. We have great leaders among us today who serve to show us that dreams can come true. We must seek to produce qualified people who will work not only for themselves but for others.

I would like to see former students become the leaders of today and take an active role in parenting their children so they can follow in their footsteps. Volunteerism and community involvement are examples of how to establish good human relationships and values.

Finally, our elders are the key component to supporting the youth of today - instilling dignity, ambition, responsibility for oneself and for his fellow man. These values are needed today as never before. We must cultivate our own system of equal rights. We must sharpen radars to detect and correct things that hinder us from being productive human beings. The U.S. Constitution states that "all men are created equal" and that all men have certain rights but history has taught us that unless we fight for these rights we will not obtain total equality. We must use these rights as tools for the task of challenging and eliminating barriers. Standing up for what you believe in and sharing it with others bridge generations. Mentoring is a good vehicle to get this point across to youth. Looking back, that hug was a moment that I will always remember.

Written by Howard Fleming

A MOST DIFFICULT TEACHING EXPERIENCE

Although I am usually an upbeat and uncomplaining instructor and professional, I will relate one of the most difficult experiences I have had while in adult education. I had been in the field for eight years and considered myself reasonably savvy as to the ways troubled learners might try to manipulate their instructor. What I was not savvy about was the manner in which staff might manipulate and pull a "fast one" on an unsuspecting (trusting?) instructor and staff member.

At the beginning of one learning session, a sub-group of four learners, ranging in ages from about 25 to about 45, entered my class as students newly admitted to the adult literacy program. Their placement in my class had been decided by one of my colleagues. On the first day of class, the four learners quickly collected at one table and proceeded to become a tightly bonded group with little respect for authority or for the learning setting. (The group was composed of three women and one man) By the beginning of the second week of instruction they clearly had made "plans" about how to embarrass the instructor (me) and distract the class. A few of the other learners became interested in their "style," and the class atmosphere began to quickly deteriorate. I did establish clear guidelines for classroom behavior, but they were clearly not interested in any such guidelines.

By the third week, they had become openly hostile toward me. (I have no way of knowing if it was the [different] color of my skin.) I then quickly went to my colleague to express my intense concerns. Soon afterward, without notifying me as to his plan, my colleague called me into his office and along with the four students. They immediately went on the attack, and he immediately proceeded to protectively defend them. Among other inappropriate measures, he began berating me for what the students were characterizing as my disrespect toward them and my inability to teach. I was aghast! This colleague then went to my supervisor with his version of what happened. No one ever, ever asked me for my version of what had happened!

As far as all were concerned, what had happened in the classroom was completely my fault. The students' version of the classroom events was totally accepted as "Truth." It was all quite humiliating and discouraging, but it was also a very good lesson for me about how I should/would never let that sort of thing take place again.

I grew up a bit that day. In the past, I had what I would characterize as some "unfair" experiences with staff, who were supposed to be there to support and work with me as part of the team. I usually took those experiences in stride, and moved on, trying to put any resentment behind me. But this particular event was so clearly directed at me on a personal level that it took me a few weeks to "digest" what had actually happened. I felt bruised! Then as I came to a clearer understanding, I realized that I would definitely address the offending staff directly if something like that ever presented itself again. It made me a more thoughtful and insightful member of a team that did not always work in concert with one another.

I am now much more watchful and pro-active when

students begin to act out in my classroom. I am also less likely to wait, hoping their behavior(s) will improve. I see that all of this is part of maturing and becoming a more effective adult literacy professional.

Written by Lois Schwait

WILLING TO LEARN

Leighanne entered the room responding to others throwing out her opinions and remarks as she took a seat away from the class. It made one wonder what had happened to her previously that caused such a response.

What is the best way to learn? Isn't that what we are continually trying to discover and what we are always talking about? Leighanne picked up on that. When we had our phonics lesson, she began making connections between our Reading Horizons Intensive Phonics program and a set of Hooked on Phonics tapes she bought for her foster children. She wondered where those tapes were. Everything was packed up in her house in anticipation of an eminent move back across country. We could imagine her going through the cardboard boxes at night to find them, confounding her housemates.

Leighanne definitely had opinions about the way and the reasons she wanted to learn. She'd rather read silently to herself. She had a tight bond with her son: a son who after a lifetime of Leighanne's academic encouragement has become her cheerleader, urging her on to earn a GED. And she knew the conditions under which she could learn; it's got to be quiet. She was not the only one in class who expressed herself in this way, but she was the one to take it seriously.

It was around this time that she began a move to the vacant, second floor of her house to have a quiet area to study and read. Little two-year-old Marty, whose life consisted of early morning bus rides and daylong attendance at a day-care center, early supper, and right to bed, fought for his time to be with Leighanne. And Leighanne fought for him to have this time. There is Little Marty, perched on the edge of Leighanne's bed strewn with books and papers, his own book in hand. There is Leighanne's brother who hardly recognizes why he lives with Leighanne and continually exposes himself to harsh criticisms delivered in a spirit of love.

Intensive Phonics starts at a very elementary level and includes penmanship exercises, which, initially, turn off seasoned students. At first this may have been the case with Leighanne. We, as teachers, were just now absorbing the core of this phonics program. Many students in the class were slow to make connections or retain the concepts. But as time went on Leighanne was right there demonstrating a thorough understanding of its application. The difference was not because she was a native English speaker and most others in the class weren't. Leighanne had her own obstacles to overcome. The difference was, she did not limit her learning to 9 to 1, Monday through Friday. She was laid off from work. She was looking forward to relocating, and she believed she could learn. Could she feel she was learning? And will she stop when she reaches this goal? There is a good chance she does, but there is a greater chance she won't.

Written by Peg Riley

Chapter 4

A CHANCE MOMENT

My journey into Adult Education came by chance, a detour so to speak, a fork in the road - the road not traveled. I was teaching middle school Special Education, and I was discouraged with the system. IEPs and the churning in and out of students, mostly Black male, who were locked into a system of labels and the realization that the "school to prison pipeline" was a real actual thing became too much to bear. So, I took a year off. I taught music to high schoolers in Baltimore City, much like Sister Mary Clarence from "Sister Act." I enjoyed my time teaching music, but the grant from Johns Hopkins ran out and I found myself jobless.

What I found was a calling and not a job. I just so happened to put on Facebook (FB) that I was looking for a job, and one of my FB friends having prior knowledge that I had some teaching experience, suggested that I apply as an Adult Basic Education Instructor. I did, and three years later and after touching hundreds of lives, I couldn't have been more certain that helping adults, especially Black women, who look like me and share the same struggles as me, is part of my life's calling. The roles are often reversed in education. The teacher is often the student, and the student is often the teacher. I am always in "student mode" because learning is a lifelong process. As the proverb says, "When the student is ready the teacher (rabbi, guru, priestess) will appear."

In Adult Education, we see many faces come and go. They come through the doors of the classroom for many different reasons. Many want to be there and many others for different reasons are forced to be there. I never judge. It is always a beautiful thing to challenge the student who may not necessarily see the value of having an education and giving them the tools to change the trajectory of their life. This change will not only affect them but future generations.

One particular student will stay with me as long I continue to do this work, and he is a constant reminder of how important this work is. His name is Dominique. He came to my class about a year ago. He had a bright smile, raspy voice, and an energy about him that spoke to me immediately. As a group, we go around the room the very first day of every session, and we introduce ourselves. We always share five things about ourselves. I always enjoy this part of the class. It gives me an opportunity get to know a lot of information about a person in a small amount of time. Dominique shared that he was 26, he has a son, and he wanted to get his GED and then enter into the Navy so that he could give his son a better life.

I took to Dominique. He was different. He was special. I encouraged him and challenged him to push himself when I felt like he was getting discouraged. I asked about his son, who I knew meant the world to him, as a subconscious reminder to keep going. We were reading *Uncle Tom's Cabin* by Harriett Beecher Stowe, and I assigned a comparative essay on two Black families from the novel. On the due date of the assignment, Dominique did not turn in his assignment. I was angry with him. I expressed my disappointment to him about his not turning in his essay. The next day he came to class. He mentioned that he could not stay because he had to go to work, but he handed me three handwritten pieces of paper torn from his spiral binder. It was his essay. I was proud of him, not necessarily because of the content, but because he did it. He honored his agreement as a student and completed the assignment. I graded his essay and returned it to him. I wanted to give him immediate feedback on his work.

That weekend, Dominique was murdered. He was shot in Fells Point in Baltimore. He tried to break up an altercation between two other men, and he was killed as a result of a gunshot to his heart. I was hurt. I still am. It felt like a loss of a brother or a son.

These streets in Baltimore are rough. They don't care if you are a young Black man trying to make it out of generational poverty and overcome illiteracy. These mean streets in Baltimore don't care if you are working and going to school to make a better life for you and your son. I read in the *Baltimore Sun,* that Dominique was a longtime lifeguard with the Baltimore City Department of Recreation and Parks, and that he had recently quit his job to focus on his education. I realized that I had a hand in that. I went to the viewing, and I finally got a chance to meet his son. I told him that his father talked about him all the time. I told his son how much his father loved him.

This article is in memory of Dominique Dungee. "On May 28, 2016 at approximately 11:55 p.m., officers responded to the 500 block of S. Broadway Street for a shooting. Upon arrival officers located 26 year old Dominique Dungee of the 800 block of N. Carey Street who was suffering from an apparent gunshot wound to the torso. Dungee was transported to Johns Hopkins Hospital where he died shortly after midnight. Investigators believe Dungee got into an argument with an unknown suspect which led to him being shot...," as reported by WBAL News.

Written by Mia Miata

THE DIVISION PROCESS

You came to me from failing schools that were so broken they could not help breaking you. You took the test and gave it back reluctantly. You were at a fifth grade level in math, so we began reviewing through division.

I wrote the steps for dividing for you. First estimate, then multiply, and if the number works, subtract and then bring down, and only then can you commence again. You only bring down one number at a time.

Equations only do exist for working out. To come out right, the numbers must line up.

I longed to say "divide yourself from what went wrong."

No number or statistic shows the damage done to ego or future. Do you recall first learning this years ago?

Please separate your work from school and life.

Don't let your pencil break or lose your place. If what went wrong could ever be deduced, there would be some remainder left to hang. Detach this place from those fluorescent halls of jeering peers.

Relax, we are different. The question now is whether you can change.

"Do you feel ready to try dividing yourself?" Such math you need to memorize by heart.

Written by Annie Shellito

All ABOARD THE LITERACY FREEDOM TRAIN

I have more than 20 plus years of experience teaching ABE/GED classes, and I still get nervous sometimes at the start of a new class cycle. Whether I am working as a part-time or a full-time instructor, I still pour the same love, high-energy, professionalism and commitment into my work. For me, it is an honor and a privilege to teach ABE/GED classes to adult learners.

Over the years, I have met some really interesting people in the field of adult literacy. From adult learners to instructors to administrators to volunteers - I have worked with some amazing and some not-so-amazing individuals. Some learners' ambivalence toward their own education and their disdain toward me as their instructor had me doubting my ability to help them succeed while the insecurities of some colleagues and/or administrators challenged me in ways that I never imagined.

I remember a situation in particular where it seemed that all of my "own" insecurities kicked in, and my efforts in the classroom seemed futile. I was stuck in what seemed like a cycle of ineffectiveness. This "stuck" feeling is something I have experienced also with some administrators whose ineffective management skills create dull and uninspired learning environments.

It wasn't until I began talking with other GED instructors and other administrators; researching best practices in the field; and reflecting on my own past experiences in the classroom that I started to get a better understanding of what I needed to do to get unstuck.

An effective day in one of my ABE/GED classes usually involved learners – either willingly or unwillingly – grasping an unknown concept or articulating their understanding of a lesson learned. A not so effective day usually meant the refusal of a learner to "go with the program" or to "buck the learning system" I had established for my classroom. Of course, my frustration would kick in and so did my ego.

She acts like she's doing me a favor by coming to class every day. Doesn't he appreciate all of the time and effort I put into preparing this lesson plan? I can't believe they took the bus tokens and then didn't show up for class.

My patience would start to wear thin, and my heart stings would feel maxed to the breaking point. Somehow just at the most opportune moment, life always seem to confront my way of thinking about my "frustrations" while causing me to remember the rebel I am.

Who are you to judge a learner for wanting to play by her own set of rules? You hardly ever do things the way other people planned, and you rarely follow the rules. So, why do you expect her to go along with "your" program?

It is true. I usually make up my own rules. Throughout the years, supervisors and even a few co-workers have complained about this character trait in me. I hardly ever color inside the lines, so why am I expecting my learners to fit nicely into the box I created for them in my classroom? I function best when I am given the space, resources and flexibility to excel. Wouldn't it make sense that my learners might function best when they, too, are given the space, the resources and the flexibility they need to excel? This question is what guides my planning and instruction.

The challenge when trying to answer this question is tackling the notion that the space and resources for any learner, particularly adult learners, to succeed might be contrary to what I have planned via "my" lesson plan. That is sometimes where the conflict begins and "behavioral problems" start to emerge.

To the K-12 educators reading this: Yes, adult literacy instructors do sometimes have to tackle behavioral problems with adult learners that often occur for some of the same reasons children act out in school. Although we don't have to deal with any adults falling out on the floor in temper tantrums; and we rarely ever have physical fights, there are rare occasions when a tense verbal exchange might happen between a student and an instructor. On those rare occasions, the instructors must make a decision as to whether or not the infraction was serious (i.e. a threat of bodily harm) or minor (i.e. disagreeable spirit). The instructors must also check their egos to be sure their response to learners is not a show of control or a way to get back at a learner for not responding in a way that instructor wanted them to respond.

I have established what I call a Clean Slate policy in my classes. I got the idea for the "Clean Slate" concept based on a quote I found on the Internet some years ago.

"Every day is a new opportunity to get right what we got wrong yesterday."

Today might not have gone well, but tomorrow is a fresh start for both my learners and me. Although my learners carry the brunt of the responsibility for their own academic success, I - as their instructor - have some responsibility, too. For this reason, I made up my mind to adhere to the following mantra in my classes:

- I will take the initiative to apologize even when I think I am right.

- I will go the extra mile with every learner, even those who seem to flaunt a chip on their shoulders.

- I will telephone and email "missing" learners on a regular basis.

- I will take the time to create a high-quality learning experience for all my learners.

- I will offer independent study opportunities that challenge all my learners to take ownership of their own learning process.

- I will relinquish my "power" as the instructor and look for ways to help learners effectively yield their own power in the classroom.

- I will research and attend professional development sessions to sharpen my craft and competency as an adult literacy professional.

- I will take the time to listen to the spoken and unspoken words of my learners.

- I will take the focus off of me as the instructor and put it back on the people that matter the most: the learners.

That last bullet point has so helped me to grow and flourish as an ABE/GED instructor. A vital lesson I have learned throughout my years of teaching ABE/GED classes is that the essence of the work I do is so not about me. Regardless of how I feel, the focal point of my work is the adult learners. I can't control how my leaners receive or react to the information I share with them, but I can control how I interact with them. I must have tough skin and a soft heart, being able to offer unconditional support even when learners don't seem appreciative. I must be willing to help connect learners to the services, supports, and opportunities they need to excel academically. I must be able to practice forgiveness, extend grace and refocus priorities on a daily basis.

If I find it too difficult or too demanding to extend compassion and flexibility to the adult learners in my classroom, then I risk becoming a hindrance to them. If learners aren't learning the way I am teaching them, then it is my responsibility to figure out a new way to teach them what they need to learn.

As ABE/GED instructors, we are all like conductors on a freedom train helping learners escape the bondage of illiteracy. This amazing journey requires immense flexibility, love, and commitment and our own willingness to take an honest look at our intent and heart for the work we do.

All Aboard?

Written by Lynn Pinder

List of Contributing Writers

(Names listed in the order submissions are printed in anthology)

Shannon Hoffman – At the time of this submission in 2009, Shannon Hoffman was a GED instructor in Hagerhill, Kentucky to native English speakers.

Kerry Murray – At the time of this submission in 2011, Murray had been teaching as an ABE Instructor at Iowa State Penitentiary through Southeastern Community College for five years.

Anonymous – This contributing writer asked to be unnamed in this anthology.

John Smith – At the time of this submission in 2016, John Smith worked as a part-time Pre-GED/GED instructor in Baltimore, Maryland at an adult literacy nonprofit organization.

Hannah M. Mills – At the time of this submission in 2009, Hannah M. Mills was an adult literacy instructor in Nova Scotia at the East Hants Adult Learning Association.

Charles F. Sleeth – At the time of this submission in 2009, Charles F. aleeth was based in Landover, Maryland and was affiliated with Fourth World Movement.

Carol McDonnell – At the time of this submission in 2009, Carol McDonnell was working as a GED instructor in Maryland at The Community College of Baltimore County.

Lin Morley Gautie – At the time of this submission in 2009, Lin Morley Gautie was based in Portsmouth, Rhode Island.

Carla Steffey – At the time of this submission in 2009, Carla Steffey was working as an adult literacy instructor in Indiana at the Hawkeye Metro Center.

Sandi L. Myrick-Nelson – At the time of this submission in 2016, Sandi L. Myrick-Nelsson was working as an adult literacy administrator in Baltimore, Maryland.

Howard Fleming – At the time of this submission in 2009, Howard Fleming was working as an adult literacy instructor in Washington, DC.

Lois Schwait – At the time of this submission, Lois Schwait was working as a part-time, Pre-GED instructor at an adult literacy nonprofit in Baltimore, MD.

Peg Riley – At the time of this submission, Peg Riley worked for the Workers' Education Program at the University of Massuchusetts Dartmouth in Dartmouth, MA.

Mia Miata – At the time of this submission, Mia Miata worked as a GED instructor at a community college in Baltimore, MD.

Annie Shellito – At the time of this submission in 2009, Annie Shellito worked at an adult literacy organization in Washington, DC.

Lynn Pinder – At the start of this anthology project, Lynn Pinder was working part-time in Baltimore, Maryland at two adult literacy nonprofits and one community college.

CALL FOR SUBMISSIONS – ABE/GED Instructors

TAKE ACTION! Publishing is seeking short creative essays (250 - 2,500 words) written by educators who have worked within the last five years as part-time and/or full-time Pre-GED and/or GED instructors of native English speakers (aged 18 years or older).

Educators can submit 250 - 2,500 word creative essays on one of the following themes:

- Funniest stories - creative essays should describe or explain one of your funniest classroom experiences as an ABE, Pre-GED or GED instructor of Native English speaking adults (aged 18 or older);

- Inspirational stories - creative essays should describe or explain one of your most inspirational experiences as an ABE, Pre-GED or GED instructor of Native English speaking adults (aged 18 or older); or

- Horror stories - creative essays should describe or explain a challenge or disappointment you faced as an ABE, Pre-GED or GED instructor of Native English speaking adults (aged 18 or older).

Submission Guidelines:

All submissions should include the following information:

(1) A cover page that includes the title of the creative essay and identifies the theme the creative essay addresses (SEE DESCRIPTION OF THE THREE THEMES ABOVE). The cover page should also include the educator's name or the word, Anonymous - to indicate that the educator wishes to conceal his/her name if his/her creative essay is selected for publication. The cover page must include the educator's email

address, the educator's telephone number, the educator's mailing address and the date. The cover page should not have a page number.

(2) A 250 - 2,500 creative essay typed in 12-point, black font and double-spaced. The educator's name and email address should be included on each page. Please insert page numbers on the first page of the creative essay. Thus, the first page after the cover page of the creative essay should read Page 1.

Please email submissions to the following address:

(Lowercase L) lpinder@thetakeactionnetwork.com

CALL FOR SUBMISSIONS – Learners/Graduates

TAKE ACTION! Publishing is seeking short creative essays (250 - 2,500 words) written by adult learners and/or GED graduates of ABE/GED programs.

Adult learners and/or graduates can submit 250 - 2,500 word creative essays on one of the following themes:

- Funniest stories - creative essays should describe or explain one of your funniest classroom experiences as an ABE, Pre-GED or GED learner ((aged 18 or older);

- Inspirational stories - creative essays should describe or explain one of your most inspirational experiences as an ABE, Pre-GED or GED learner (aged 18 or older); or

- Horror stories - creative essays should describe or explain a challenge or disappointment you faced as an ABE, Pre-GED or GED learner (age 18 or older).

Submission Guidelines:

All submissions should include the following information:

(1) A cover page that includes the title of the creative essay and identifies the theme the creative essay addresses (SEE DESCRIPTION OF THE THREE THEMES ABOVE). The cover page should also include the name of the ABE/GED learner/graduate or the word, Anonymous - to indicate that the learner/graduate wishes to conceal his/her name if his/her creative essay is selected for publication. The cover page must include the email address, the telephone number and the mailing address of the learner/graduate. The cover page

should also include the date. The cover page should not have a page number.

(2) A 250 - 2,500 creative essay typed in 12-point, black font and double-spaced. The name and email address of the learner/graduate should be included on each page. Please insert page numbers on the first page of the creative essay. Thus, the first page after the cover page of the creative essay should read Page 1.

Please email submissions to the following address:

(Lowercase L) lpinder@thetakeactionnetwork.com

Visit http://takeactionpublishing.blogspot.com to view other books published by TAKE ACTION! Publishing!

www.ingramcontent.com/pod-product-compliance
Lightning Source LLC
Chambersburg PA
CBHW021920040426
42448CB00007B/833